SUN
SHINE
SPACES

BECI ORPIN

hardie grant books

Contents

Introduction

So, here we are – my fourth DIY book! How lucky am I? And even luckier considering that in this book I get to focus on one of my favourite things: the outdoors. Although, it wasn't always that way.

As a child, I spent a healthy amount of time outside, usually barefoot, exploring nature and then obsessively recording everything I saw (spotting a pink heath wildflower was a particular treat). As I got older, I was less the 'outdoors type' and more the 'nocturnal type'. In my twenties I worked in nightclubs and, with my social calendar as my first priority, the only daylight I usually saw was the sun rising as I went to bed and then setting as I got up.

When my kids arrived, these habits were swiftly broken. With a new baby in tow, I saw a lot more daylight – and night time come to think of it – than I had in years. I found myself pushing the pram around my local park and wandering around the botanical gardens near where I lived. It may have been new-mum delirium, but these walks rekindled my love for nature. I began to marvel at the abundance of flora and fauna right in the heart of the city: black cockatoos, fruit bats, flowering gums ... I had always considered nature an inspiration, but this discovery of urban nature became a particular point of fascination and a source of new inspiration for me.

These days, my kids are grown and I'm back to working regular hours, but my love for urban nature only grows stronger. Some days I'm at my desk, often for hours on end, tapping away at my computer or foraging through piles of art supplies, when I find myself longing for the halcyon days of park-pram-pushing. It's a reminder that I have to force myself to get outside as much as I can. Riding my bike is a good way to do it, as is cruising around our neighbouring parks, and I'll never pass up a swim in the ocean once the warmer weather arrives. (But, as a side note, my outdoorsy-ness definitely stops at camping. I camped with my dad when I was younger, but I fail miserably when it comes to doing the same with my family. Glamping, however, is totally acceptable!)

Through these ebbs and flows of nature involvement, I've come to the conclusion that the more time I spend outdoors, the happier I am. 'Sunshine Space' is the term I use to describe this happy nature place, and I thought it would be a good idea to make a book about it. In the pages that follow, you will find a bunch of outdoors-inspired projects to make and ideas to try, to encourage you to get outside and into nature – and maybe you'll even create your own Sunshine Space.

INDOORS

14

It might seem strange to start a book about the outdoors with a chapter based around the indoors, but bringing the outdoors into the indoors can make your indoors so much better. First of all, there is the seemingly everlasting indoor plant trend. There's a good reason that trend has stuck around: indoor plants rule! They are good for your mental health and physical wellbeing and, quite simply, they look great. And who doesn't love living in a jungle?

Then there are pets; they are outdoor 'things' that we sometimes like to bring inside. Where would we be without those guys? I know I'd be completely lost without my two feline friends, which is why I made a project just for them in this chapter. Read on for other great ideas on how to bring the outdoors into your indoors.

15

YOU WILL NEED:

- various interesting pieces of nature: leaves, small sticks, branches, gum nuts or seed pods (these may be fresh or dried/pressed, but dried leaves hold the paint better and last longer)
- paper and pencil
- paint (I used pink and white)
- small pots or containers for the paint
- small paintbrushes
- small round stickers
- embroidery thread (I used pale pink and white)
- PVA glue
- pins
- natural wooden beads
- white sewing cotton
- ready-made round scarf hanger (or wire to make your own), or a 25 cm (10 in) length of 1 cm (½ in) wide dowel

NATURE MOBILE

Most of the time, nature is just too good to mess with. But occasionally, adding a tiny splash of paint and a few polka-dot stickers can take it to a whole new level. A level that makes you want to make a mobile from your extra-prettied-up nature, hang it on the wall and admire it for a long time.

That being said, if you do choose to pretty up nature, make sure your decorations add to, but don't overwhelm or take away from, the natural beauty of the object itself.

NOTE: Nature is very original and you probably won't be able to find exactly the same pieces of nature that I did, so this project will be impossible to replicate exactly.

The steps on pages 20–21 show a variety of techniques that you can apply to make your own interpretation of a nature mobile.

It's also a good idea to stick to a very limited colour palette so as not to overwhelm nature's own colours.

19

Arrange your pieces of nature on the table. Look at their size, shape and form, and work out roughly which pieces sit well together. You could also write a plan or sketch a few ideas of the techniques you will use on each piece.

Technique 1, Paint dip: Pour some paint into a small pot, then dip a stick or small group of seed pods halfway into the paint. Hold until the paint covers the immersed part of the object. Remove from the paint, holding the object over the pot, to allow the excess paint to drip off. Put aside to dry, making sure the painted area is not touching any surface.

1 /

2 /

20

3 /

4 /

Technique 2, Using a paintbrush: Use a small paintbrush to apply paint to your leaves, sticks or seed pods. Try painting a simple stripe or pattern, or paint half the leaf, leaving the other half unpainted. Choose a pattern that is sympathetic to your chosen object.

Technique 3, Adding stickers: Add small round stickers to give a random polka-dot effect.

Technique 4, Binding sticks together: Break the sticks into smaller lengths, then arrange into shapes. Use three sticks to form a triangle and four for a square or diamond.

Bind the sticks together by winding embroidery thread around them until they hold fast. Tie off the end or secure with a dab of glue applied with a pin. You could also add a wooden bead and let it hang down in the centre, or sit a bead on top (secure it in place by knotting the thread at the top).

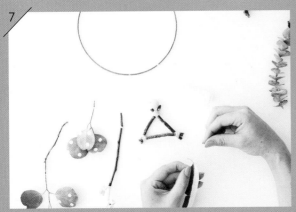

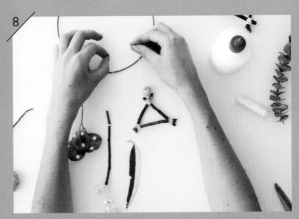

Once all your mobile pieces are complete, attach lengths of white cotton to the top of each one by wrapping it around the object and then securing with glue. Make sure you leave ample cotton at the top, to attach the pieces to the wire or dowel.

Attach all the elements to the wire or dowel. Adjust the position and length of cotton so everything is hanging freely, then wind the cotton around the wire and secure with a knot and a dab of glue. If using dowel, add a length of embroidery thread to the top, for hanging.

22

23

Foraged flowers

I'm not sure if it's because I'm rapidly approaching middle age, but I have a new-found love of growing flowers. I am yet to do it very successfully, although I have had a few glories in the red salvia department.

My grandmother was a keen gardener and only now do I fully appreciate how wonderful her garden was, filled with azaleas, daphne, roses and the occasional patches of pink, purple and white cosmos. I think there's nothing more satisfying than picking flowers from your own garden and arranging them in a vase in the kitchen or on an occasional table (my gran had lots of those) – and it's a lot more environmentally responsible. I recently looked into the environmental cost of flower farming – that shiz is pretty cray, and seems ridiculous when flowers actually grow for free all around the place.

I was also inspired to look for flowers further afield after seeing my friend Katie Marx's photos on Instagram. Yes, she is an incredible florist with a long list of stellar clients, but seeing her gathering beautiful wild things on a country roadside was definitely another lightning-bolt moment: YOU DON'T HAVE TO PAY FOR FLOWERS! From then on, whenever I spotted some Queen Anne's lace by the roadside, I would yell at Raph to pull over and then make him and the kids get out to gather up armfuls of beauty from nature's free flower shop. The best!

But we can't, and don't, all have gardens, and we don't all take regular road trips to the country. If that's the case, then foraging for flowers in an urban environment is a skill you can learn.

All the flowers in the photos on the next few pages were foraged from the inner city, either from nearby parks, bushes hanging over back fences or pathways, or kind donations from neighbours' gardens. Even though, to my knowledge, it's not technically legal, I have been known to roam the neighbourhood on summer evenings, with a pair of snips in one hand and a beer in the other, chopping away at overhanging rose bushes.

But really, you don't want to be stealing from other people's gardens. People with beautiful gardens usually have put in a bunch of hard work to get them that way, so it's not really fair to snip away at their flower bushes (particularly at midnight, with a beer in hand). But, it is okay to take them from parks (in moderation, and as long as it isn't from a national park … obviously!) and from your friends', families' and neighbours' gardens, too – with their permission of course.

Foraging for flowers means you have to look at flora somewhat differently. Don't think about traditional cut flowers – tulips, gerberas, carnations and the like – as the chances of finding them on a forage are pretty slight (unless you're in Amsterdam). But you will find beautiful natives (flowering gum – SQUEAL), grasses and weeds. Yes, weeds – weeds like the aforementioned Queen Anne's lace can make the most beautiful arrangements – and grandiose cut branches can look dramatic and breathtaking. Anyone would think you have a personal florist! One of my favourite things ever was finding a bunch of small oak branches that had been cut off during a council tree trim. It was early spring so they had budding, yellow-green leaves on them. I carried them home and put them in water and they lasted for weeks.

26

27

28

30

YOU WILL NEED:

· flowers/foliage: ones with flat petals are best (see a list here: www.preservedgardens.com/pressed_flowers.htm).
I like pansies, geraniums, flowering weeds – anything pretty and dainty
· book/iron/microwave: what you use will depend on which method you choose
· paper or card: try blotting paper, coffee filter paper, printer paper, several layers of tissue paper

NOTES:

· Flowers should preferably be freshly picked, to prevent browning.
· Don't pick your flowers too early in the morning, as they will still have dew on them. The extra moisture from the dew may cause them to go mouldy during the pressing process.
· Flowers should have just bloomed or be about to bloom. If they are too mature, they will lose their petals.
· If the flowers have obvious stamens, remove them before pressing.

32

PRESSED FLOWERS

I am an avid collector of many things, but old books are one of my favourites – I rarely walk out of an op shop without one. Quirky typesetting and old-school printing aside, one of the things I love about second-hand books is the chance of discovering a little surprise inside them. I've found many treasures tucked inside those yellowing, musty pages, including some flattened Easter-egg wrappers from the 1940s, a birthday note from an aunt to a favourite niece and, best of all, several books containing some beautiful pressed flowers.

When I was a child I used to press flowers with my grandma, and I remember never having enough patience to wait the weeks and weeks before the flowers were completely dried and pressed. Luckily for me, while I was researching this project, I discovered that there are several methods of pressing flowers, some of which allow you to cheat, so you don't have to wait forever and ever before they are ready. This is good news for me, as I still have as much patience as a five-year-old.

Method 1, Pressing in a book: (This is the easiest but slowest method; I found it produced the best results.) Open up your book and place a sheet of paper on one side of the book. Liquid from the flowers can leach into the surrounding pages, so use an old book or several sheets of paper to prevent this. **TIP:** Don't use a phone book, as the paper is too flimsy.

Arrange your flowers on the piece of paper, making sure the flowers aren't overlapping (unless you want them to). Cover with another piece of paper (or fold the first piece of paper in half) and close the book.

34

Weight down the book by placing some heavy books or bricks on top of it.

Change the papers after 1 week, then leave for a few more weeks until the flowers are completely dry. Try to resist the temptation to check them (unless changing the paper), as this can disturb the flowers.

Method 2, Ironing: Flatten the flowers between pieces of paper in a book, following steps 1–3 (left). Leave the flowers to dry for however long you can manage (I recommend at least 1 day). Empty any water out of the iron (you don't want any steam), and set the heat to the lowest setting.

Remove the flowers from the book, leaving them sandwiched between the two pieces of paper, and press them with the iron for 10–15 seconds. You don't need to move the iron around, just press it on the paper.

35

Method 3, Microwave: Arrange the flowers in the book between two pieces of paper, following steps 1–2 (left). Make sure that your book has no metal in the spine or type before putting it in the microwave. Place in the microwave and zap for 30 seconds. Take the book out and let it cool by opening the pages to let the steam out (don't open the pages that have the flowers enclosed). **TIP:** Have a couple of books on the go at once, so you can have one heating in the microwave while the other one is cooling down.

Once the book is cool, zap it in the microwave again. Repeat until the flowers are almost dry (you may need to do this about four or five times: smaller flowers will dry out quicker), taking care you don't overcook them, as the flowers will turn brown.

36

38

39

Indoor plants

In my dream house, I would have a sun-lit room just for plants. My friend Sally Wilson has one of these. She lives in an inner-city apartment, carved out of a beautiful old building. It has a small sunroom and a well-protected deep balcony dedicated entirely to her plants. The first time I spent an afternoon drinking tea in this glorious space, I was ready to move in. Yes, the high ceilings and period details of the building were impressive, but it was the plants that elevated it to the next level. The contrast of the lush greenery against a background of the sirens and noises of a very urban location made it feel even more special.

Inner-city jungle room aside, Sally has something else that I don't have: a great deal of know-how in keeping her indoor plants happy and healthy. Sally works with and writes about plants – her knowledge is deep. Admittedly, my thumb is not completely black. I manage to keep more indoor plants alive than kill them, although my plant patience won't extend to the fickle (I'm looking at you, fiddle-leaf fig). The more plants I own, the better I seem to get at keeping them alive.

The main thing I have learnt during my indoor plant adventures is what plants work where. This has taken some time, having lived in my house for the better part of a decade, but I now know where a hoya will thrive (upstairs bathroom), where the rubber plant likes to live (hated the lounge room, loves the sunroom), and which room will kill anything (freezing weird cave room with no lights – even mother-in-law's tongue couldn't survive there). If you live in a rental or are often moving (as I was up until we bought our current house), then deciphering this can be tricky. To help, I have compiled a list of my favourite fail-safe plants (see pages 44–46), the ones that I have successfully kept alive in my home and studio for at least one year.

40

42

43

Chain of hearts (also known as string of hearts and rosary vine)
(*Ceropegia woodii*)

These are possibly my most favourite indoor plant – I love the delicate trailing leaves so much! I have three at home – one in my bedroom (good light), hallway (low–moderate light) and sunroom (moderate light) – and they are all thriving. I pay them very little attention (apart from admiring their cuteness as I walk past), water them occasionally, and they just keep going.

LOVES: Any light it can get, but will grow faster with more light.
HATES: Overwatering, so make sure it's in a pot that has good drainage.

Devil's ivy
(*Epipremnum aureum*)

I have a few of these around my studio; one particularly huge one is growing up a stump and is slowly taking over everything. The studio has relatively low natural light but good artificial light, and these guys just keep on growing. I have occasionally forgotten to water them too, and it's only when the leaves start to sag that I remember they might need a drink. But give them a good soak and they bounce back easily.

LOVES: Low–medium light, moderate watering, leaves being wiped down with a wet cloth.
HATES: Nothing. This plant is very easygoing.

Dracaena
(*Dracaena fragrans*)

This is one of those plants that you can literally forget about for months and it will be okay. I know this because we have one in our warehouse in the staff bathroom, which is not used very often. I go to this bathroom probably once a month and there it is, still going strong. I'll give it a little water, it gives me some 'thank you' plant vibes, and then I won't see it for another month. Our relationship works out great with this set-up.

LOVES: All round neglect. Does best in bright light, but will tolerate any conditions.
HATES: Overwatering, direct sunlight, attention.

Hoya (also known as wax plant)

My gran's house had one of those old-school sunrooms, like a covered porch that wrapped around the house. From memory it was full of the best '70s décor: large cane chairs, frilly cushions and lots of plants. This is where I came across my first hoya plant. Hers was a decent size and was covered in pink waxy flowers, and my four-year-old self just could not get my head around how those flowers were actually real, because they looked so fake! Years later, my head still boggles with this thought, but it's part of the reason why I love hoyas. They come in lots of different varieties, often distinguished by numbers. I have a no. 12 hoya in my bathroom, which is growing rapidly, and a Curly Rope hoya in my lounge, which is growing very slowly but looks incredible.

LOVES: You can find a hoya for almost any condition, so each will have its individual needs. Research before you buy.
HATES: Will not flower in low-light conditions.

44

Mother-in-law's tongue

(*Sansevieria trifasciata*)
These guys are known for their indestructible nature, BUT I have killed a few. Now I know this is from overcrowding – this guy loves a lot of space in the pot. We currently have one in the windowless bathroom of our doughnut shop and it's going great, so it obviously can deal well with artificial light. We also have one on our warehouse landing and it's doing okay too, though I think I'll move him to the warmer surrounds of the office soon. These plants are also great air purifiers.

LOVES: Will do okay in any moderate temperature, but it is a desert plant so it thrives where it's warm, but never in the direct sun.
HATES: Too much water – let it dry out in between waters; overcrowded pots.

Peace lily

(*Spathiphyllum*)
I've had many of these guys over the years and they have always fared well. Currently, I have one at home, which has lived in many different locations: our freezing cold front room, our sunroom and our bedroom. Basically I just put it anywhere and then when it looks unhappy I move it to a different location. It seems to cope with this peripatetic lifestyle pretty well. It does like to be watered though, but will tell you if it's thirsty with droopy leaves.

LOVES: Weekly watering. Most places, but will do best in slightly warmer areas (but not too hot). Will flower in warmer temperatures.
HATES: Not being watered.

Philodendron

These guys come in many different shapes and sizes. I have a medium-sized one on my studio table, which seems to be getting bigger every time I look at it. So far it seems to love the artificial light it gets. I also have a large one in our warehouse, which was very sad and neglected, but after some intensive care it looks like it's going to make it through. I have one in my lounge (*Philodendron maximum*), which is doing okay, but not loving life that much. I might have to move it.

LOVES: Low–medium indirect light (but will do well in artificial light), moderate watering, leaves being wiped down with a wet cloth.
HATES: Direct sunlight.

Rubber plant

(*Ficus elastica*)
During my plant-shopping adventures, I never gave the rubber plant a second look until I was given one in a pale pink pot; the combination of the dark green leaves against the pretty pot had me positively salivating. Now it's one of my faves. At first I put my rubber plant in our low-light lounge room, but after a while the leaves seemed to be dropping off a bit too quickly. I moved it to a spot in our sunroom, which was warm but with no direct light, and now it's sprouting new leaves like there's no tomorrow!

LOVES: Bright indirect light and moderate watering (**TIP:** you're watering it too much if the leaves start to turn yellow and drop off). These guys can be fickle, but find the right spot and they will thrive. Leaves need to be wiped down with a wet cloth.
HATES: Being moved around, colder temperatures, draughts.

45

Spider plant
(*Chlorophytum comosum*)
Another plant that thrives on neglect and is very easy to grow. We have one in our doughnut shop; it doesn't get a whole lot of loving, yet it keeps on growing. I had the same plant in my studio for a while, and the lack of light in there almost killed it, but once it was moved into the brighter light downstairs it soon returned to full health.

LOVES: Well-drained soil, bright light, cooler temperatures.
HATES: Heat and overwatering.

Succulents/small cactus
I have a bunch of different varieties on my lounge room windowsill; I love them because they look like a group of sculptures. They grow slowly (if at all) and ask for very little in life. You will need to experiment with different varieties to see which ones work best indoors. Most of them need some kind of sunlight or warmth, but overall they are pretty hardy.

LOVES: Good drainage and warmer temperatures.
HATES: Overwatering.

Let it be known:
There are lots of other great indoor plants out there. These are just the ones that have worked best for me. Also, be aware that some plants are toxic to pets. If this concerns you, or if your pets are particularly partial to eating plants, make sure you do some research first to check what indoor plants are the most pet-friendly.

46

47

49

50

51

Natural dyeing

I have dabbled with dyes for quite a while now. There are dyeing projects in all of my previous books but way before then, when I was studying, the art of mixing dyes was something we were thoroughly tested on. I learnt that dyeing is a true art form, one that I loved but probably didn't master.

I loved messing around with dyes, but was often put off by the chemicals. Chemical dyes are so toxic – you have to wear a mask and often safety glasses when preparing them, as they can easily irritate your eyes and mouth. And that's just on a domestic level. On a commercial level, the textile industry is the main source of pollutants in the world, much of that from dyeing fabric, which is kinda insane. Anyway, I'll get off my eco high-horse now.

My interest in natural dyes prompted me to take part in a workshop with Belinda Evans, a weaver who specialises in using native flora to dye the yarns for her weaving. Her workshop was brilliant and gave me lots of great info to then go forth and start my own adventures in using natural dyes.

I decided to experiment with things that were really easy to find: things that you might have in your pantry, could easily buy at the supermarket, or find in a park or your garden. There are lots of great natural dyes too, such as indigo and cochineal that produce beautiful long-lasting colours, that you can order online.

After doing lots of research online, I realised there are many variables that can affect the result of natural dyes (or any dyes for that matter):
· the freshness of the ingredients (the dye stuff or dye matter)
· the amount of ingredients you use to prepare the dye
· the source of the ingredients (for example, acorns from a tree in a city park might dye fabric a slightly different colour than acorns from a tree in the middle of a forest)
· the temperature of the water and how consistent that water temperature is
· the amount you agitate the fabric
· the type of mordant.

It's honestly endless, but that's all part of the fun of experimentation. Bear in mind also that carrying out these experiments is a waste of time unless you keep some kind of record (even just a rough one) of what you've tried and the results.

Because they don't rely on chemicals, natural dyes generally produce much subtler colours, although there are some exceptions: behold the glorious tones of turmeric. Often natural dyes, especially ones from vegetables, don't hold well in fabrics and fade quickly, even without the sun. But there are also exceptions to the rule.

Natural dyes will only be effective on natural fibres – think cellulosic fibres (from plants), such as cotton and linen, and animal-based fibres, such as silk and wool. I tried my dye tests on cotton, linen and silk. Silk took the dyes the best in all my tests (they achieved the deepest and strongest colours).

When it comes to experimenting with natural dyes, part of the fun lies in making your own discoveries and finding your own way to do things. However, before starting, it's a good idea to familiarise yourself with the basic process (see page 55).

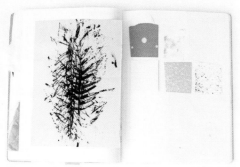

54

1. Fabric pre-treatments and mordants

All fabrics should be washed first to remove any sizing or finishes. The fabrics then need to be prepared with a mordant. A mordant is something that fixes the dye to the fabric, so the dye doesn't run out when it is washed.

BASIC MORDANTS

Basic mordants are either acid or alkaline. The general rule is to use:

· acid for cellulosic fibres (plant based, such as cotton and linen);
· alkaline for protein fibres (animal based, such as silk and wool).

But rules are made to be broken so, in the interests of creative experimentation, I tested all my fabrics in both acid and alkaline mordants.

· For the acid mordant, I used 1 part white vinegar to 4 parts water.
· For the alkaline mordant, I used 1 part cooking salt to 16 parts water.

Put your fabric in a pot with the mordant and simmer for 1 hour.

RUSTY NAILS MORDANT

I also used a mordant of rusty nails for my experiment with the acorns, but this needed a bit of advance planning.

· To make the mordant, I placed 10 rusty nails in a glass jar with around 500 ml (17 fl oz/2 cups) of white vinegar. I left the jar until the liquid turned orange (sunlight will aid the process) – mine took about 2 weeks.
· You then make the dye by boiling the acorns (as for all the other dyes). Once you have the dye, add the rusty vinegar (the colour will change from brown to black), then add the fabric. Simmer the fabric in the dye for 1 hour.

2. Preparing the dye

While your fabric is simmering in the mordant, prepare the dye. There are so many things that you can use to make natural dyes – the possibilities for experiments are infinite. Pages 56–58 show some of the items I used to prepare the dyes, and the results. Next on my list of things to try are berries, saffron, rusty nails, Queen Anne's lace and other flowers.

Once you've gathered your material (dye stuff), you need to chop it if it's large, and add it to a saucepan of water. I used a pot with a 5 litre (1⅛ gallon/20 cup) capacity. Bring the liquid and dye stuff to the boil, then reduce the heat and simmer gently for 1 hour.

TIP: The dye can stain your pot, so it's a good idea to buy a cheap one from the op shop. A heavy-based pot is good, and copper is even better, if possible (the copper also acts as a mordant).

3. Dyeing the fabric

After simmering for 1 hour, the dye should be extracted from the ingredient. Strain off the dye stuff, reserving the dye liquid in the pot.

Wearing gloves and using kitchen tongs, remove your fabric from the mordant and rinse under cold water (take care, as the fabric will be hot). If you removed the fabric from the mordant a while ago and it has now dried, rinse it under water. Place the wet fabric in the dye liquid, making sure the fabric is completely submerged in the dye.

Bring the liquid to the boil, then reduce the heat and leave the fabric in the simmering liquid for 1 hour, constantly agitating the fabric with a stick to get an even colour result. If you are dyeing wool, you need to check it regularly to make sure the wool is not felting (this is why I didn't use wool for my experiments).

If you like, take the pot off the heat and leave the fabric in the dye for an hour or so, overnight or for a longer period to achieve a deeper shade. When I did my tests, if the fabric wasn't dyed a deep colour after 1 hour, I then cut the fabric in half, took one half out and left the remainder in the dye overnight.

Again wearing gloves and using kitchen tongs, remove the fabric from the dye. Rinse under cold water until the water runs clear. Leave the fabric to dry out of direct sunlight.

55

Here is a list of ingredients I used for my experiments, and the results. Use these as a rough guide for your own tests – who knows what you'll discover!

Acorns

DYE STUFF:
About 200 acorns (sounds like a lot but it's not!).

METHOD:
Added to a standard pot of water and simmered for 1 hour.

RESULTS ON FABRIC:
I added a rusty-nail vinegar mordant to the dye (the colour changed from brown to black as soon as I added the mordant) and then added the fabric, and left it to dye for 1 hour. Produced a beautiful soft grey colour (it was supposed to be black!).

NOTES:
There is no need to presoak the fabric in a mordant when using acorn dye, as acorns already contain a natural mordant.

Avocado

DYE STUFF:
About 35 avocado stones, which I collected from a taco truck.

METHOD:
Added to a standard pot of water and simmered for 1 hour.

RESULTS ON FABRIC:
Produced the most beautiful shade of pale pink. The colour was slightly more brownish on silk. I left the silk in the dye for 2 hours (simmered for 1 hour and then left in the pot for 1 hour), and the cotton and linen for 6 hours.

NOTES:
When preparing the dye, you could try adding the avocado skins as well.

Beetroot

DYE STUFF:
6 medium beetroot (beets), cut into small pieces.

METHOD:
Added to a standard pot of water and simmered for 1 hour.

RESULTS ON FABRIC:
Produced a very pale pink when left overnight. Same results with a salt/vinegar mordant.

NOTES:
Beetroot often stains your hands more than the fabric! Wear disposable gloves if you don't want stained hands, and use an old plastic cutting board when chopping the beetroot (wooden boards are very porous and any stains will be hard to remove).

Dandelions

DYE STUFF:
Half a pot of dandelions (not chopped, only washed to get rid of the dirt from the roots).

METHOD:
Filled the rest of the pot up with water and simmered for 1 hour.

RESULTS ON FABRIC:
Had very little effect; there was a slight beige discolouration after 2 hours of dyeing.

NOTES:
I gathered dandelions from my friend's garden – and this helped with weeding at the same time! I didn't use the flowers as there weren't any in bloom at the time, but using the flowers would (reportedly) be more effective and should produce a light yellow dye.

Grass

DYE STUFF:
Half a pot of grass (not chopped, only washed to get rid of the dirt from the roots).

METHOD:
Filled the rest of the pot up with water and simmered for 1 hour.

RESULTS ON FABRIC:
Dyed for 2 hours with very little effect. The silk went a few shades darker, but there was no change to the cotton and linen.

NOTES:
Different types of grass will produce different results: experiment with various fabrics and grasses to see what works best.

Hibiscus

DYE STUFF:
200 g (7 oz) dried hibiscus.

METHOD:
Added to a standard pot of water and simmered for 1 hour.

RESULTS ON FABRIC:
Produced a purplish-brown colour after 2½ hours of dyeing.

NOTES:
You can also use fresh hibiscus for dyeing, although dried hibiscus is much easier to use and find. You can buy dried hibiscus flowers from herb and spice stores and Middle Eastern grocery stores.

Red cabbage

DYE STUFF:
½ small red cabbage, chopped into small chunks.

METHOD:
Added to a standard pot of water and simmered for 1 hour.

RESULTS ON FABRIC:
Very light purplish-brown when dyed for 2 hours; turned a pretty darker lilac when left overnight.

NOTES:
The dye washed out easily and was affected by sunlight (I left it out to dry for one day in a shaded area and it still faded).

57

Red onions

DYE STUFF:

6 red onion skins, chopped.

METHOD:

Added to a standard pot of water and simmered for 1 hour.

RESULTS ON FABRIC:

Produced a pretty brownish-pink colour after dyeing for 2 hours. A deeper shade was achieved after leaving the fabric in the dye overnight.

NOTES:

You can also dye with brown onion skins – this should give a lighter shade of brown.

Turmeric

DYE STUFF:

4 tablespoons ground turmeric.

METHOD:

Added to a standard pot of water and simmered for 1 hour.

RESULTS ON FABRIC:

Produced an amazing bright yellow. Simmered for 1 hour, then turned off the heat and left it in the dye for 2 hours.

NOTES:

The dyed fabric can be left smelling of turmeric. If this bothers you, try airing the dried fabric out for a day, or wash in cold water with a small amount of washing powder.

58

Once you've dyed your fabric, it can be used in endless ways. I made cushions with mine, but pillowcases, scarves, bags and even garments are all great ideas. If you have dyed yarn, use for weaving, knitting or pompoms.

And please be aware that some dyed fabrics may fade faster than others, so it's best not to use them for outdoor items. I found that fabrics dyed with beetroot and cabbage faded fairly quickly when left outside, but those dyed with avocado and turmeric did not.

59

YOU WILL NEED:

- circular saw
- pencil and ruler
- 2.4 x 1.2 m (94 x 47 in) piece of 12 mm (½ in) plywood
- round template, about 20 cm (8 in) in diameter
- electric drill
- jigsaw
- medium-grit and fine-grit sandpaper

- cloth or rag
- PVA glue
- twelve 30 mm (1¼ in) screws, or a hammer and twelve 25 mm (1 in) nails
- scissors
- offcuts of industrial felt or carpet, or anything that has a good surface for cats to scratch (natural jute rope is also an option) – enough to cover one side of the pyramid, 50 cm (19½ in) square

Cushion
- pins
- 2 pieces of durable fabric, about 35 cm (14 in) square
- large circle template, about 30 cm (12 in) in diameter
- sewing machine and thread
- cushion stuffing
- needle and thread

Pompom
- wool
- pompom maker

PET PYRAMID

I have two cats: Miso and Tio. Miso has the typical FU cat-nonchalance. Everything we give him is greeted with an ungrateful meow, except for food – as soon as he sees food, he pushes us out of the way so he can scoff it down. On the other hand, Tio – who has his faults too – loves whatever he is given. Give him a toy mouse and he will happily play for hours; give him a cushion and he will promptly sit on it and stay there all day. So when our friend generously donated a deluxe cat's scratching pole, Miso ignored it, but it quickly became Tio's favourite thing ever. However, this time I sided with Miso. That thing was an eyesore. In fact, most things in the cat's scratching pole genre are hideously ugly, which can be tricky for us cat-loving, aesthetically minded people.

And so the Pet Pyramid was born. The Pet Pyramid is pleasing to the eye, is functional and Tio-approved (which is not that hard). It is also suitable for small dogs, such as this cutie in the photo. If you are using this for your cat, consider placing it up high. Cats love the security of being able to watch everything from a high place.

NOTE: For ease of cutting the mitred edges, this project uses a larger sheet of plywood than needed, so there will be some wood left over.

Using the circular saw with the blade tilted 30 degrees inwards, mitre along one of the long edges of the plywood panel. Then, with the blade still tilted inwards, cut out a 50 cm (19½ in) wide strip down the length of the plywood, ensuring the two mitred edges are facing inwards.

With the blade of the saw tilted back to a right angle (or 90 degrees), cut the strip into three panels 50 cm (19½ in) long. You should now have three 50 cm (19½ in) square panels, each with two mitred edges.

64

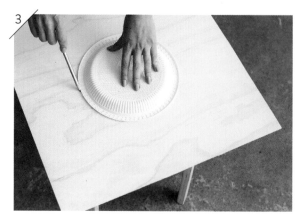

Take one of the panels and draw a circle in the centre for the 'peep hole'. I used a plastic plate as a template for the circle. **TIP:** Cats will not go through any opening that their whiskers won't fit through. The average length for a cat's whiskers is 20 cm (8 in), but if your cat has particularly long whiskers, make the hole bigger.

Drill a hole at the edge of the circle to start you off.

Cut around the marked circle with the jigsaw.

Use the medium-grit sandpaper to sand all the edges of the panels until smooth. Sand around the inside of the hole. Dust off with the cloth.

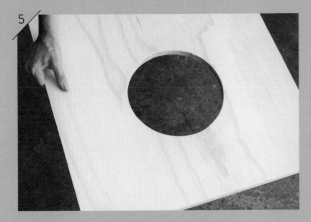

Glue the panels together to create the pyramid. Make sure you match the angles of the panels as shown.

Add some screws using the electric drill, or use a hammer and nails to secure the panels in place. Use fine-grit sandpaper to sand all the surfaces and edges, then dust off with the cloth.

Cut the felt to size and glue it to one side of the constructed pyramid (the side without the peep hole). I used three strips of felt in different colours.

Cushion: Pin the two squares of fabric together. Using your template, draw a circle onto the fabric about 30 cm (12 in) in diameter. Cut out two circles from the fabric, adding a 1 cm (½ in) seam allowance all round.

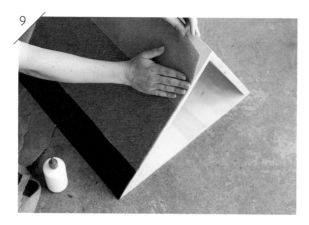

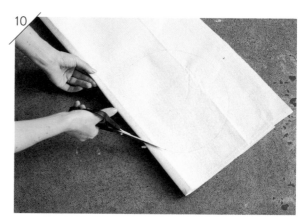

66

Pin the right sides together. Sew around the edge, leaving a 10 cm (4 in) opening. Turn right side out and fill with the stuffing. Close the hole with hand stitching. **TIP:** Don't overstuff the cushion. You want it fairly flat so your pet doesn't knock it out on their way in and out of the pyramid. The cushion will also flatten out the more they sit on it (especially if your pets are rather 'big boned' like mine).

Pompom: Wind the wool around the pompom maker and, once full, cut the wool. Place some string (I used a length of wool) around the cut wool, then pull it tight and tie a knot to keep in place. Trim your pompom and hang it at the entrance to the pyramid.

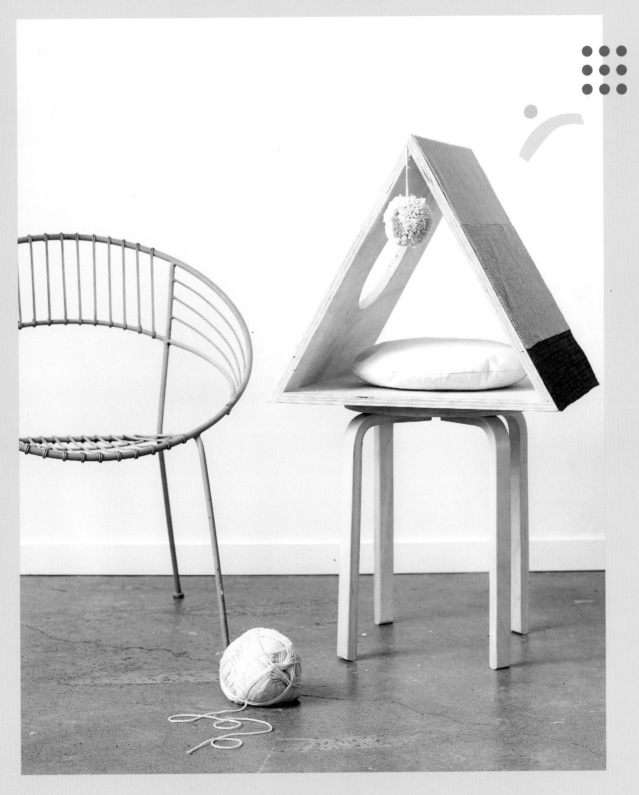

OUTDOORS

I love spending time outdoors, but my job means that I'm often stuck indoors. I can't tell you how many times I've wistfully looked out my office window at a beautiful sunny day, while frantically working with a deadline looming. Sometimes life can be so unfair.

In this chapter you will find projects that you can make inside, to then maximise your enjoyment outside (well, you could make them outside but, in my experience, craft and outdoors usually aren't a great mix). Don't have a backyard to use them in? No stress! These projects are suitable for all outdoor situations, whether it be a tiny balcony, a park or beach. The important thing here is to make sure you get outside and use them once they are finished.

73

YOU WILL NEED:

- 1 small (approximately 8 kg/18 lb) bag of white cement (I made 5 pots)
- water
- safety glasses and mask
- stick or spoon to mix concrete and colours
- containers: old containers for mixing concrete; a selection of plastic containers and pots to use as moulds; small containers to place in the middle to create the opening
- acrylic paint
- scissors
- potting mix
- small trowel
- plants

76

CONCRETE PLANTERS

During my apartment-living early twenties, I managed to accumulate a pretty good collection of potted plants. Along with our masses of records and books, these were the most pain-in-the-arse things to move – and I did move frequently back then (my record was four times in one year).

Amid this process, there were always a few moving victims: smashed pots, which left poor, bare-rooted plants behind! And being constantly on the move also made me poor, so I had to use odd vessels to temporarily house these poor homeless plants until I could afford to buy new pots. Had I known then how easy and cheap it is to make pots from concrete, I would have been doing that in the blink of an eye. Anyway, now I do know, and although I can now afford to replace broken pots, it's way more fun making your own, especially when you can make them almost any shape and colour you like.

Mix up the concrete following the instructions on the packet. I didn't add the suggested sand, to get a finer finish. Pour the concrete into separate containers (if you want three colours plus one white, divide the concrete among four containers). **WARNING:** Concrete dust is toxic! You must wear safety glasses and a mask.

Add paint to your containers of mixed concrete. Note that when the paint and concrete dries, the colour will be considerably lighter, so go for a darker shade rather than a lighter one.

78

Choose your mould containers and pour in some cement as a base colour.

Add different layers of different colours, or use one colour for each pot. When the container is full, use a stick or spoon to swirl the concrete around a little – this will produce a slight marbled effect between the layers. **TIP:** Don't fill the container right to the top or the concrete will overflow when you insert the container in the centre in step 5.

Insert a smaller container into the middle of your filled mould container to form the opening of the planter.

Put some rocks in the centre of the smaller container to weight it down. Don't weight it down too much, or it will touch the base and the planter will end up with a very thin (or no) base. Leave the concrete to harden. The longer you leave it to dry, the better the results (I left mine for about 1 day).

5

6

7

8

Once completely dry, carefully remove both the outer and inner containers. You may need to use scissors to cut away the edges of the container.

Add potting mix and a plant to your concrete pot.

YOU WILL NEED:

· scissors
· aluminium camping chair
· 200 m (219 yards) of 4 mm (⅛ in) rope (I used nylon paracord): 100 m (109 yards) white, 50 m (55 yards) grey, 25 m (27 yards) yellow, 25 m (27 yards) pink

· 2 size Q crochet hooks
· Macramé Chair template, page 186
· lighter or box of matches

NOTE: Create a 'skein' for your cord (this could be a long, thin piece of card or plastic). Wrap your cord around the skein and unwind it as you go. This will make it easier to handle the cord when passing it through the other cords.

MACRAMÉ CHAIR

This was definitely the most laborious of all the projects in this book. I not only tested mountains of different ropes and cords to get the right one (nylon paracord maintained the right amount of tautness when woven, and is also suitable for outdoors), but perfecting the crochet knot took a few goes as well. And once that was decided, I laboured over patterns and colours. But, good things come to those who wait (or persist), and I feel like I ended up with a pretty amazing chair.

Don't let these instructions scare you; they may seem complicated at first, but this is one of those projects that becomes clearer once you actually start doing it. And when you do, it will only take a few knots before it will start to become second nature. Before you know it, you'll be sitting in your chair on your lawn, with a cocktail (or mocktail) in hand, enjoying the result of all your hard work.

If you do need some extra help along the way, you can find some great video tutorials by searching 'macramé chair tutorial' on YouTube.

81

Using scissors, cut and then pull off the existing webbing from the chair.

Vertical cords: Using the white cord and starting from the bottom left of the chair, tie a double knot around the frame.

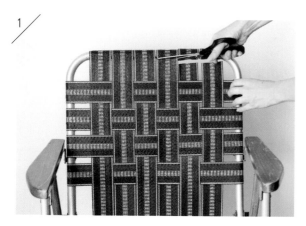

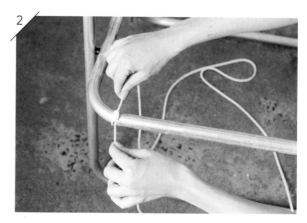

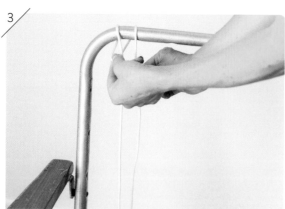

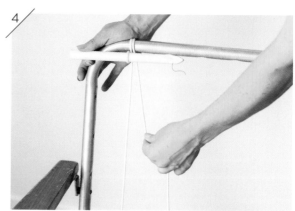

Pull the cord through the seat of the chair, behind the centre back brace bar and up to the top left side of the frame. Make a loop in the cord at the top bar. Pull the loop behind and then under the bar and over to the left.

Insert your first crochet hook in the loop, with the hook pointing towards the right side of the chair, and pull the cord tight so the hook rests against the chair frame. Bring the cord back down under the centre back brace bar to the front.

Create a loop in the cord on the bottom chair frame, then pull it over the front of the bar and behind to the left.

Insert the second crochet hook into the loop and pull the cord taut. The hook will rest on the chair frame.

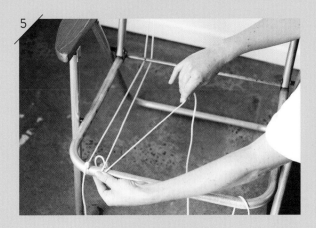

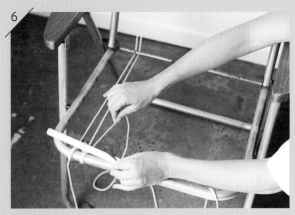

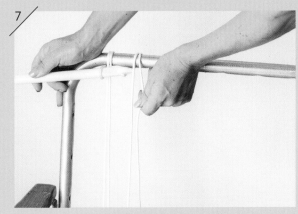

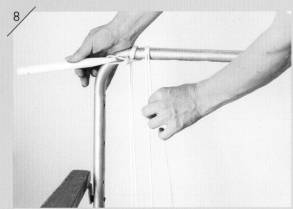

Pull the cord through the seat of the chair, behind the centre back brace bar and up to the top frame. Make a loop in the cord at the top bar. Pull the loop behind and under the bar and to the left of the last vertical cords you created.

Hook the new loop over the crochet hook. The existing loop on the hook will overlap the two vertical cords to its right.

Pull the loop taut, then pull it through the loop you made in step 3. This will create a chain stitch. Rest the crochet hook in the loop.

Pull the loose cord down behind the centre back brace bar and to the front. Create a loop, then pull it over the top of the front bar.

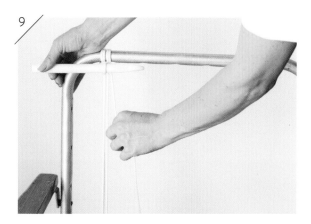

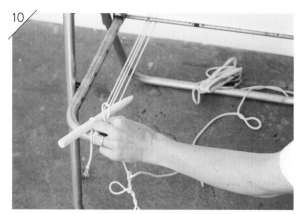

84

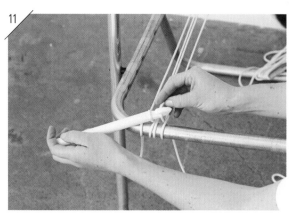

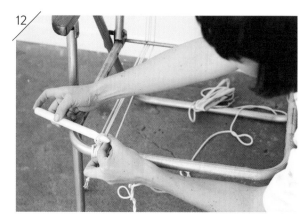

Pull the loop around the top bar and to the left of the last vertical cords you created. Hook the new loop with the crochet hook.

Pull the new loop through the loop created in step 6, making a chain stitch. Pull the loose cord taut.

Repeat these steps until you have 40 knots and have filled the top and bottom bars with taut cord. To finish, cut the cord off the skein, making sure you have about 1¼ m (4 ft) left. Pull the cord through the last loop and remove the crochet hook. Pull the cord behind the back brace, over the front bar and through the loop on the other crochet hook.

Horizontal cords: These are completed using the same method. Follow the Macramé Chair template, starting with 3 knots of white followed by the grey cord to form a semi-circle pattern.

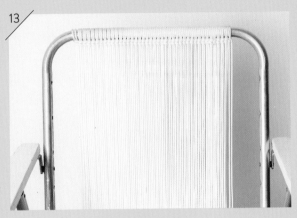

Continue with the pink cord to form the second half of the circle.

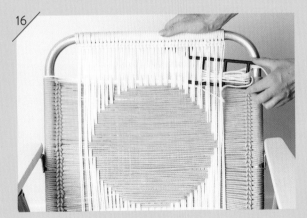

Finish with 3 more knots using white cord. Repeat on the base of the chair, using the yellow and grey cords. To finish, simply tie off the cord. Use a lighter or matches to burn the end of the cord to ensure it does not fray (you can do this with all loose ends).

YOU WILL NEED:

- white outdoor umbrella
- pencil
- disposable gloves
- dark blue fabric dye (or use fabric paint or fabric markers)
- old container for mixing up the dye
- paintbrush

90

SUN UMBRELLA

In my dream life, I have a pool with all the accessories, plenty of sunshine and lots of time to enjoy all of these things. This, of course, is still very much a dream, but in the meantime I thought I could make some part of this scenario a reality by creating my ideal sun umbrella. It's definitely much cheaper than getting a pool.

You don't need to copy my pattern if you don't want to – get creative and make your own pattern. You could just keep it simple with polka dots, or classic with stripes.

91

Open out your umbrella and draw your design on the fabric.

Wearing gloves, mix up the dye following the packet instructions.

1/

2/

92

3/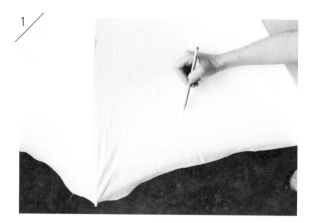

4/

Paint the dye onto your pencilled design. Don't load your brush up with too much dye or it will drip. Take your time – don't rush it! If you aren't feeling confident, practise on a piece of plain scrap fabric.

Once the design is completed, let it dry (this won't take long, but can vary depending on the type of fabric). Heat-set the dye following the packet instructions.

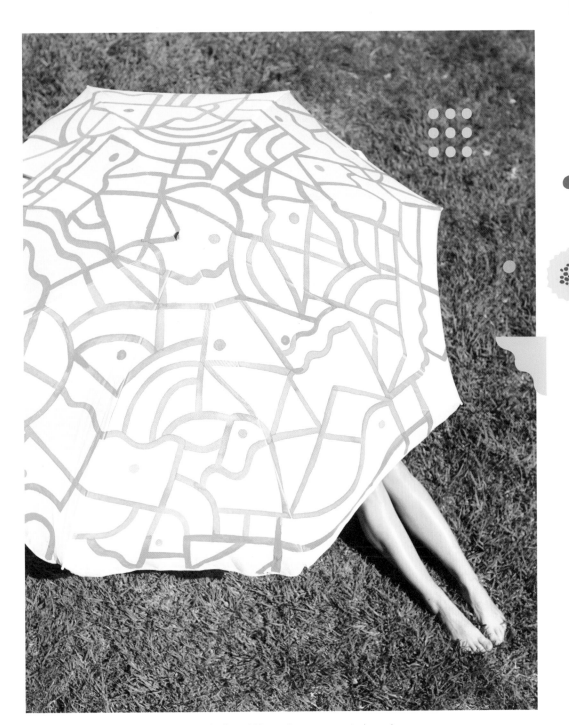

93

Place your umbrella poolside – or in a sunny spot in the garden.

94

YOU WILL NEED:

- waterproof or plastic-backed cushion fabric (see Note, below)
- scissors
- wide paintbrush (or a small paint roller)
- smaller paintbrush
- acrylic paint
- pencil
- round template and/or ruler (depending on the shape of your cushions)
- pins
- sewing machine and thread
- cushion stuffing (polyester-based is best for outdoor use)
- needle and thread

OUTDOOR CUSHIONS

My quest to find perfection in outdoor comfort has been a long one. All the outdoor cushion options seemed to be boring, ugly and just plain uncomfortable. After a while, logic prevailed and I made my own, and it was so easy and pretty cheap, too. Now I have a set of cushions perfect for backyard picnic soirees, the beach, or pretty much any outdoor sitting occasion.

Because the fabric is painted, the cushions do feel a bit crackly and rough at first, but they will soften up over time. These cushions have a plastic backing on the inside, so offer protection from the damp ground. But I don't think they would handle long-term exposure to the elements, so take them inside when not in use – they'd make great indoor floor cushions as well.

NOTE: For the cushion fabric, I used a plastic-backed canvas drop sheet (bought from a hardware store) that measured 3.6 x 1.5 m (12 x 5 ft). This was enough for the four cushions shown at right: one 65 cm (25½ in) square, two 50 cm (19½ in) square and one 50 cm (19½ in) round (there will be fabric left over).

97

Cut your top fabric roughly to size, leaving about 10 cm (4 in) allowance over final size. Using the wide paintbrush, paint the base colour on the fabric side of the material. You don't want the paint to be too thick – water it down slightly if it is. **TIP**: Using a roller to apply the paint will make it easier to apply a thin layer.

Once the base coat is dry, draw your design onto the fabric.

1/

2/

98

3/

4/

Using a small paintbrush, paint the design. Leave the paint to dry thoroughly.

Mark out the final size and shape of the cushion using the pencil. For the round cushion, use a circular object such as a sunhat or plate as a template (remembering to accommodate for seam allowance). If you are making a square cushion, measure and mark out the desired size. Mark out the fabric for the base of the cushion at the same time.

Pin the painted top fabric and the plain base pieces together. Following the pencilled lines, cut out the two pieces of fabric together.

Pin the right sides together (the plastic sides should be facing out, so they end up on the inside of the cushion). Sew around the edge on a sewing machine, leaving a 10 cm (4 in) opening for the stuffing.

Remove the pins and turn the cushion right side out. Fill the cushion with the stuffing.

Close the hole with hand stitching.

101

YOU WILL NEED:

- 2 m (6 ft 7 in) of 140 cm (55 in) wide strong canvas fabric
- pins
- sewing machine and thread
- tape measure
- pencil or fabric marker
- scissors
- 22 rivets, 23 mm (1 in) in diameter (plus a rivet tool, which should come with the kit)

- mallet or hammer
- 66 m (72 yards) of natural rope (ensure this is good quality and load bearing), plus extra rope for hanging
- 2 metal hoops or carabiners strong enough to handle appropriate weight

Pompoms
- wool to match the canvas fabric (I used black and white)
- pompom maker

CANVAS HAMMOCK

The experience of lazing in a hammock in a shady spot on a warm summer's day, with a book in one hand and a cool drink in the other, has got to be one of the best things about being human. You can feel even more smug/gloaty with the thought that you've made the hammock yourself. And guess what – it's actually really easy!

There are lots of DIY hammock projects out there. Some are very simple, involving just a few bits of rope and some fabric, both tied in knots – but those ones terrify me! We grew up with a hammock like that in our backyard, and although no serious injuries occurred, it came pretty close once or twice. So, in the interests of public safety, this hammock is both easy to make and safe to use.

Fold a 4 cm (1½ in) hem at each end of the fabric. Pin in place and sew.

Mark out where the rivets will go on the seam. I used 11 at each end, spaced about 11 cm (4¼ in) apart. Using scissors, make small holes on the marked points. Following the instructions on the packet, attach the rivets using the rivet tool and the mallet. **TIP:** I placed a wood offcut underneath the canvas, to protect the work surface.

106

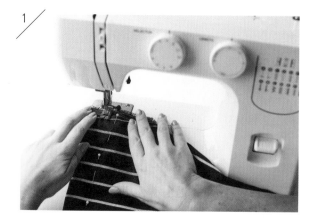

Cut the rope into twenty-two 3 m (9 ft 10 in) lengths. Fold each rope in half and thread it through each rivet using a cow hitch knot to fasten (see step 4).

To form a cow hitch knot, insert the folded end of the rope through the hole and then pull it through to form a loop. Push the two rope ends through the loop and pull to tighten the knot (see the diagram on page 186).

Once all the 3 m (9 ft 10 in) lengths are attached through the rivets, gather all the rope at one end and tie it into one large knot. Repeat for the other end. This might need adjusting once it is attached to the hanging space.

Pompoms: Wind the wool around the pompom maker and, once full, cut the wool. Place some string (I used a length of wool) around the cut wool, then pull it tight and tie a knot to keep it in place. Cut this piece of wool, leaving ample length for hanging. I made two white and two black pompoms.

Attach the lengths of wool left on the pompoms to one end of the hammock (or attach two on each end).

To hang the hammock, attach the ropes on each end to a metal loop or carabiner with a double knot (make sure the knot is very tight so the hammock is secure). Attach extra rope to the other side of both carabiners and then tie that rope around a tree or somewhere else sturdy enough to take the weight.

PARTY

I've said it before and it will be said again: I am a bit of a hedonist. Maybe even a lot of a hedonist. In fact, fun could be my religion, making throwing a party my equivalent of going to church on Sundays. Okay, so it's not usually weekly, but more often than not, we spend our time entertaining. As our house is small in the entertaining-space department, having parties outside is something I am somewhat expert at. There's nothing better than taking the party outside on a warm summer's night, but even when the weather turns cold, there is still fun to be had.

We are pretty no-fuss when it comes to entertaining, but there are a few things I like to do to make an occasion a little more special. I've included some of my best party tips here, so you can add a little bit of 'special' to your outdoor parties, too.

111

YOU WILL NEED:

- florist wire or thin wire
- wire snips
- a variety of flowers and foliage: choose different shapes, textures and colours but make sure they complement each other (I used gyp/baby's breath, sedum and pink hypericum berries)
- scissors
- floristry tape
- washi tape, preferably green (optional)

FLOWER CROWN

Is there anything that says 'summer, come at me!' more than a flower crown? I think not. Flower crowns have also been a mainstay in music-festival fashion for the past few years, but you could make a flower crown for any reason or any season (check out my wintry bay leaf version on page 150).

We have gone for a crazy, over-the-top crown here, using a fairly simple collection of flowers, but with maximum volume potential (all hail gyp!). I'd say this floral beauty is more suited to a spring afternoon tea party rather than bouncing around at a festival, but it's up to you. And I'm pretty sure Frida Kahlo (the queen of all flower-crown wearers) would approve, too.

NOTE: Think about how long the flowers you are using will last. Choose flowers that are hardy and do well without water (all my choices do). If not, make the crown as close to wearing time as possible.

Wrap the wire around the desired position on your head. Once the wire is the correct width and shape, loop it another two or three times around your head. Cut with wire snips and fasten the end by wrapping it around the wire loop a few times.

Sort the flowers into small groups and cut the stems into manageable lengths. Start to wrap the stems of each small flower bunch with the floristry tape.

1 /

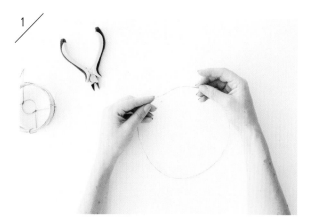

2 /

116

3 /

4 /

TIP: It can take a while to get used to using floristry tape. It is not adhesive, but binds through stretching, winding and the heat from fingers, which makes it mould together. It can be fiddly, so do a few practice bunches before proceeding with the final ones.

Wrap the tape around four bunches to start with.

Add two bunches to the left side of the wire, spacing them about 2 cm (¾ in) apart and facing the flowers to the front. Secure the bunches to the wire by wrapping floristry and washi tape around the wire and bunch ends. Repeat, adding two bunches to the right side.

Make a few more bunches and add them to the wire. Add as many bunches as you like, until you are happy with how the crown is looking.

5/

6/

117

7/

8/

TIP: Try the crown on as you go. It can look completely different when it's on your head from how it looks on a flat surface.

When the crown is finished, I like to add a final layer of green washi tape over the ends of the bunches to keep everything securely in place. You might also like to wrap the washi tape around the wire crown, to give it more structure. If you aren't wearing the crown straight away, store it in the fridge or a cool place.

YOU WILL NEED:

- A2 card or paper: 1 sheet each of pale pink, grey and white (I used 220 gsm, but anything between 110 gsm and 240 gsm will be suitable)
- black ink and blue ink
- mouth atomiser (from art and craft stores) or old toothbrush
- protective clothing, such as plastic gloves, apron and safety glasses
- scrap paper
- small spray bottle filled with bleach
- small spray bottle filled with water
- small paintbrush
- Paper Crystals templates, pages 187–189
- scissors (or ruler, craft knife and cutting mat)
- tool for scoring
- double-sided tape or paper glue
- pin

122

PAPER CRYSTALS

The most fun I had with this project (aside from admiring the beautiful finished product) was experimenting with different paper treatments. I had no idea that bleach could change grey paper to a beautiful pink shade, or to mint when I tried it on a different type of grey paper.

There are three crystals here and I used a different paper treatment on each one. Three look nice together, but if you enjoy making them, they would look amazing en masse as an outdoor table centrepiece. These also look wonderful when it's dark if you sit a small lantern inside them – even the crystals made with a heavier weight card will still produce a lovely soft glow when lit from inside. Try experimenting with different papers: heavy-weight tracing paper could look particularly beautiful.

Also, a shout-out to Nyssa Skorji for the technical developments on this project. Nyssa created the crystal templates from scratch and is a paper genius!

Paper treatment 1: Place the pale pink card on your table. Using black ink and the mouth atomiser, create a fine mist of ink splatters over the paper. Alternatively, you can create a fine spray by dragging your thumb over a toothbrush dipped in ink. **TIP:** This is messy (wear gloves and an apron) and can take a few goes to get it right.

Paper treatment 2: Lay down some scrap paper and place the grey card on top. Take the spray bottle filled with bleach, adjust the nozzle to a fine spray and spray bleach over the card. The sprayed area should change colour almost immediately. **WARNING:** Be very careful when spraying the bleach. I recommend wearing protective clothing, including gloves and safety glasses.

124

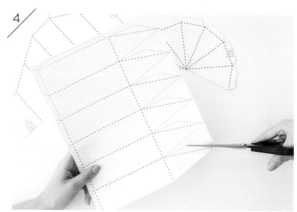

Paper treatment 3: Take the spray bottle filled with water and lightly spray the white card. Using the paintbrush, work some blue ink into the wet areas so the ink spreads and fans out in different ways. Leave to dry. The card may need flattening once it has dried. If so, place it under several heavy books and leave it to dry completely, preferably overnight.

Copy and enlarge the Paper Crystals templates. Cut them out with scissors or, if you are handy with a craft knife and ruler, use those for more precise results.

Place the templates over the treated cards and cut them out. If it's easier, you might like to trace around the templates first, and then cut them out.

Score the cut-out card as indicated by the dotted lines on the templates. **TIP:** For scoring, use a ballpoint pen that has run out of ink; or you could use a craft knife, applying very light pressure so you don't cut the card all the way through.

5/

6/

125

7/

8/

Fold the cards and fasten with double-sided tape or glue, as indicated on the template. Use a sewing pin to add pin holes to certain areas (this will let more light through).

Attach the top of the crystal to the bottom, adding glue or double-sided tape to the tabs. Gently press down to secure in place (you will need to put one hand inside the crystal to support it, pressing down with your other hand on the outside at the same time).

126

127

YOU WILL NEED:

- black-and-white printouts of photos, or vintage copyright-free illustrations of vegetables, flowers, fruit and insects (choose an assortment of shapes and sizes)
- watercolour paints
- watercolour brushes
- scissors
- white card for backing and stands
- double-sided tape
- paper glue
- sticky tape
- craft knife and cutting mat
- assorted papers and cards (in plain colours and patterns such as stripes, grids and small polka dots)

TABLE COLLAGES

We often have people over for dinner, but because our dinners are usually quite casual we never have allocated seating. In fact, more often than not we invite more guests than can fit around the table, but that's nothing that a plate on a lap can't solve. BUT if we did allocate seats, then I'd use these collages as name plates.

Elaborate yes, but let's face it, I'm usually not the one doing the cooking, so I've got time to put together these little numbers pre-dinner. Plus, they are super fun to make, look great on the table and then everyone gets to take them home as a keepsake of the evening (if you're willing to part with them, of course).

Colour your black-and-white copies using watercolours (I like painting things in unnatural colours – a blue broccoli or a pink cauliflower).
TIP: The black-and-white copies have a lot of black toner on them, which resists the paint. That's okay, just keep painting.

Roughly cut around the painted copies and then stick them onto the white backing card.

130

TIP: I used double-sided tape to stick mine onto the card, but glue works just as well.

Cut around the edge of the image. You may need to use a craft knife to cut around the detailed areas.

Cut out some shapes from the coloured and patterned cards. I used shapes such as crosses and circles, but you can use anything as long as the shapes and colours complement your images. Play with the position of the images until you are happy with their arrangement.

Once your arrangement is final, secure with double-sided tape and glue. Use glue for securing the smaller areas and double-sided tape for the larger ones.

131

Turn your paper collage over and add some sticky tape on the back to secure everything in place. You might also like to add a plain card or paper backing (use your collage as a rough template and cut out a plain piece of card that will cover the back).

For the stand, cut out two small triangles from the white card. Starting at the top, cut a slit halfway down the triangle. Repeat for the second triangle. Cut two slits the same length into the base of the collage, one on the left side and one on the right. Insert the triangle stands into the slits. Adjust if it does not stand up evenly.

YOU WILL NEED:

- pins
- sewing machine and thread
- iron
- plate or similar for round edge template
- pencil or fabric chalk
- scissors
- needle and thread

Fabric for the front:
- 4 pieces of fabric to make a total of 200 x 160 cm (79 x 63 in). I used fabric offcuts in contrasting colours and patterns:
  - 2 pieces of fabric 120 x 80 cm (47¼ x 31½ in), plus 1.5 cm (½ in) seam allowance (grey stripe/black mini dot)
  - 2 pieces of fabric 80 x 80 cm (31½ x 31½ in), plus 1.5 cm (½ in) seam allowance (black stripe/solid beige)

Fabric for the back:
- 205 cm (81 in) square piece of waterproof backing (see Note, below). Cut to 200 x 160 cm (79 x 63 in), plus 1.5 cm (½ in) seam allowance

For the bind (edge of blanket):
- 810 cm (319 in) of 2.5 cm (1 in) wide cotton herringbone tape. This is the total amount needed if you are using all the same colour.

However, I used:
- 250 cm (98½ in) in pale blue
- 70 cm (28 in) in yellow
- 130 cm (51 in) in pink
- 250 cm (98½ in) in grey
- 110 cm (43 in) in off-white

For the handle:
- 140 cm (55 in) of 4 cm (1½ in) wide stiff ribbon or similar

PICNIC BLANKET

My quest to find the perfect picnic blanket has so far proven fruitless. We've tried and tested so many: a woollen blanket with a cool leather strap = too scratchy and not machine washable; a woven plastic one with cool ethnic vibes = too bulky and not machine washable; and a good ol' tarpaulin = wipeable but too plasticy and not machine washable. So instead, I've decided to make my own ideal picnic blanket: cute, comfy, waterproof, transportable AND machine washable!

NOTE: I found a rubber-backed nylon rip-stop, which was perfect, in a remnants store. It was also 220 cm (87 in) wide, so I didn't need to sew two pieces together to get the right width. But if you can't find any extra-wide fabric, sew two pieces together.

Pin the four pieces of fabric together for the front. Sew them together leaving a 1.5 cm (½ in) seam allowance.

Iron all the seams flat. If your fabrics are cotton or linen, use the hottest heat setting.

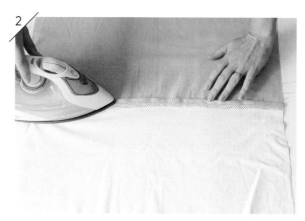

134

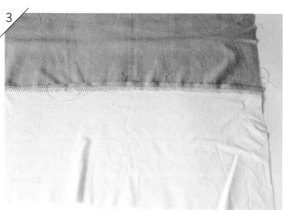

Lay the waterproof backing piece out flat, with the rip-stop side (the right side) facing up. Place the fabric front piece on top, right side facing down. (When the blanket is turned the right way out, the waterproof or rubber side will be hidden inside the blanket, but will still stop the moisture getting through.)

Pin the front and back pieces together around the edges. Pin a row along the front middle seam as well, to prevent the two pieces from moving around.

Make sure the fabric is lying flat, then use a plate (or similar) as a template and mark out a rounded edge on all four corners.

Pin the edges, leaving a 1.5 cm (½ in) seam allowance and sew around the edge, leaving one corner – about 35 cm (14 in) – unsewn so you can turn the blanket the right way out later.

135

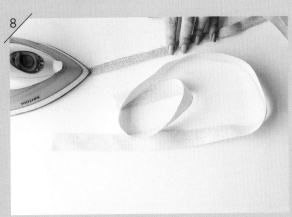

Trim off the marked rounded edges. Turn the blanket right side out through the space left unsewn. Iron flat and then hand sew the gap to close it.

To make the bind (edge of blanket): If you are using different colours, sew the lengths of tape together on a machine, end to end, to form one long piece. Iron in half all the way down the length.

Fold the bind around the edge of the blanket so there is half on either side of the edge. Pin in place and then sew.

For the handle: Cut the ribbon into two 55 cm (21½ in) long pieces and one 30 cm (12 in) long piece.

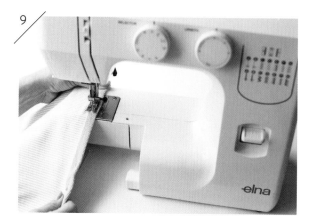

136

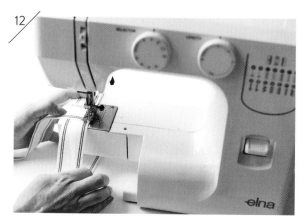

Fold each 55 cm (21½ in) piece of ribbon into a loop, with a 4 cm (1½ in) overlap. Pin each loop in place and then sew.

Attach the two ribbon loops to each end of the 30 cm (12 in) piece of ribbon. To do this, place one loop at one end of the ribbon, then fold the end of the ribbon under the loop. Pin and sew in place. Repeat with the other loop. To use with the blanket, fold the blanket in half and then in half again. Roll it up and then slip the rolled blanket through the loops (as shown on the right).

137

Meadow picnic

Despite the fact that my kids are city kids, they still need open spaces to run and throw frisbees and to do all the things that kids like to do. I often say – in the nicest possible way, of course – that my children are like dogs and need to be taken for a run every day. Even though we live in a Victorian house with a typically long, narrow, small yard, we are blessed with a large park opposite our house, so there's open space aplenty.

Another thing our long, narrow, badly arranged house is not so good for is kids' parties. We've had a few good goes at it, but quickly discovered there is no worse hell than twenty or so five-year-olds buzzed up on ice-cream cake and lemonade, bouncing off the walls of our small lounge room. Throw in a few live reptiles (whose idea was that?) and … let's just say it didn't end well (although no reptiles or children were harmed in the process – it came close though).

So, for our sanity and our kids' greater enjoyment, outdoor parties it is, and hence the evolution of the Meadow Picnic. Why Meadow Picnic? Well, it seemed like a vague enough theme, no dressing up is required (although you can if you want to), and it's not hard to find a meadow – in the form of a backyard with long grass (ours!), a local park or not-too-far-away paddock, if you have one nearby.

In a world where kids' parties have gone Pinterest-board crazy, I like to keep things low fuss and low cost, but with enough cute details to make it feel like a special celebration. In my experience, children don't care too much about the decorations or theme; as long as there are lots of kids, a few organised activities and a bit more sugar than usual, they are happy.

For our Meadow Picnic, I used things we already had, plus some extras that I found at an op shop. For a colourful and comfy seating area, I layered lots of tablecloths on top of each other, and threw in a few cushions for comfort. I also bought a few metres of solid-colour cotton and gave it an extra meadowy touch by adding a leaf print. This was surprisingly easy to do.

I used a small roller brush and some black acrylic paint, rolled the paint over a leaf, and then pressed it onto the fabric. I experimented with a few different leaf types on paper beforehand, to see which worked best.

Next, a few quick dress-up ideas. Fresh flower crowns: I cut crowns from stiff craft card and fastened them together with tape, then made small slits around the crown, picked a few flowers and inserted them into the slits and then fastened them on the inside with tape. So cute! I wanted to wear one. I also bought some thin plastic headbands and then wrapped some floristry wire around the top of them, shaping the wire into bunny and fox ears. To finish it off, I wrapped some coloured washi tape around the wire ears and voilà – animal ears! You could also make bee antennae, adding polystyrene balls on the end.

I wanted to add a touch of 'meadow' to the food as well. I put edible flowers on top of cupcakes (you could also freeze edible flowers into ice cubes if you are organised enough), and made faux mushrooms using cut red-apple tops toothpicked together with a marshmallow bottom. I also made some bunny and fox strawberry holders from the same craft card as the crowns, with faces drawn in black marker. These could be used for chocolates or any other small treat, and make cute party favours too.

And then games, again keeping it old-school and simple. Here are some meadow-inspired games to play:

· hide and seek
· scarecrow tiggy
· apple bobbing
· ring around a rosie
· sack races
· tug of war
· scavenger hunt.

After all that food and fresh air, you should have some partied-out kids ready for an early night. Get the wine ready!

142

144

Equinox dinner

I get particularly emotional about the change of seasons. I have been known to weep at the beauty of an autumn sunset, or revere in the joy of the first warm night of spring or summer by throwing impromptu, outlandish backyard parties. Pretty much any excuse to celebrate nature and the change of seasons and I'm on it. Thus evolved the Equinox Dinner. I love a bit of a pagan celebration too, so this idea ticked all the boxes for me.

As with all celebrations, I like to keep things pretty no-fuss, but still put in enough effort to make it feel special. My Equinox Dinner had to be outdoors – what's the point of celebrating the moon if you're not sitting under a moonlit sky? And, in keeping with the pagan tradition, we held our dinner on a full moon, but any time, weather permitting, is A-okay.

I decided this would be an adult-only celebration, with my guests arriving at dusk. I used my cousin's incredible garden for this occasion, but anywhere with a bit of space, some grass and trees is ideal. Think your local park or field or ask a friend if you can use their backyard (depending on the size of your guest list).

First of all, there were the table decorations to consider. I had a 'woodsy' palette in mind: black, white, neutrals, wood and dark green. To fit in with my pagan theme, I wanted guests to be seated on the ground around a low table. I created mine with two long trestle table tops supported by several milk crates. Swathes of white tablecloths were definitely part of my vision, and for these I used bed sheets and a few long white tablecloths that I bought from an op shop. I asked guests to bring cushions to sit on, and cut a huge plastic-backed drop sheet into two strips, to go on the ground on each side of the table, for extra comfort and so the cushions wouldn't get dirty.

Table decorations were minimal; there was no need for flowers when we were surrounded by such beautiful foliage and greenery. The primary focus for the table was the masses of candles, in different shapes and sizes. This was the part I splurged on, but it was absolutely worth it – candlelight is both magic and perfect for an outdoor dinner party. I grouped the candles on pieces of cut logs, which I borrowed from my local florist, although I had to be careful not to forget about the candles as the night wore on, as I didn't want to start any fires! You could achieve a similar effect with rustic wooden breadboards, or take a wooden log to your local hardware store or timber mill and they should be able to cut it into thin slices for you.

I also made a quick 'phases of the moon' centrepiece with black-and-white cards on wooden skewers, poked into long pieces of balsa wood to keep them in place.

I'm not a fan of dress-ups (unless it's for my kids and then I'm all over it), but I did ask my guests to stick to a black-and-white theme when dressing, and they happily abided.

I also made some bay leaf crowns for everyone to wear – an ode to the beautiful Scandinavian Santa Lucia crowns, which also have lit candles added, but I wasn't brave enough or responsible enough to go that far. Bay leaf crowns are easy and cheap to make. I ordered a bunch of bay leaf branches from my grocer (you can also order them from florists), bent them into shape and bound them together with floristry tape (see page 116 of the Flower Crown project for tips on using the tape). I also made a few ivy crowns, as there happened to be some ivy growing in the garden – and why not? To my surprise, everyone loved wearing the crowns. It added an extra layer of both beauty and folly to the party, and they smelt great, too.

The menu was also suitably rustic and pagan-esque (prepared by Raph, under my direction) and was kept no-fuss: roasted meats (and roasted beets for the vegos), simple fresh salads and, of course, lots of wine. I was going to make cocktails but wine (and ale) seemed more apt. Next time I would decanter the wine into some Viking-looking vessels, but pouring it straight from the bottle looked fine as well.

And, finally, there were fairy lights – lots of them! Although fairy lights have suffered much decorating overkill in the past, for this occasion they created the perfect atmosphere as the sun went down and the party continued on into the wee hours. But remember, unless you're set up close to a house and a source of power, you'll need to make sure your fairy lights are battery operated.

In my dream pagan celebration, there would have also been some star watching, a huge bonfire and a mock virgin sacrifice. Unfortunately, a cloudy night, fire restrictions and sensible publishers told me this was a no-go. And it was pretty perfect as it was.

148

150

PLAY

The combination of kids and outdoors is a no-brainer. Well, it is for my kids anyway. Yes, they need to expel all that excess energy that children tend to have, but it's more than that. With the amount of child-alluring technology on offer these days, it's too easy for kids to stay indoors in front of screens. Outdoor play can teach kids the art of discovery, independence, resilience, problem solving and a host of other life lessons that can't be gained from screens.

It was with this in mind that I came up with the projects in this chapter – all designed to get kids out of the house and interacting with the outdoors in one way or another.

YOU WILL NEED:

- scrap paper
- four 3 m (10 ft) lengths of white fabric, about 1.2 m (4 ft) wide (I used varying weights but all lightweight fabrics, such as gauze or poplin)
- acrylic paints: grey, mustard, pale pink, navy (or use fabric paints if you have them)
- wide paintbrushes
- scissors
- pins
- sewing machine and thread
- retractable knife
- 6 m (20 ft) of 20 mm (¾ in) wide flexible cream-coloured irrigation tubing
- 3 irrigation tubing joiners
- tape measure and pencil
- 8 m (26 ft) of 3 mm (⅛ in) rope or cord, cut into four equal lengths

HIDING SPACE

How much do kids love a hiding space? For that matter, how much do adults love one, too? I love it when my kids create their own spaces to hide in, but I don't love the mess left afterwards. I feel like I'm folding up sheets and putting away cushions for days.

This is a hiding spot you can make that is somewhat more permanent, and can be quickly collapsed and put away for another day. It can also be moved outdoors and lined with blankets and a few cushions, to provide a comfy, shaded reading/napping/tea-party spot for both kids and adults alike.

Cover the work area with some scrap paper, then place your first length of fabric on top. Have all your paints ready.

Using a wide paintbrush, paint large waves and swirls on the fabric. If you don't have enough space to lay the whole fabric length on the table, paint sections and then, when it's dry, move the fabric along to the next blank spot.

1 /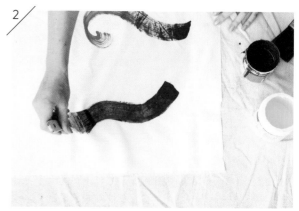

2 /

162

3 /

4 /

Use a variety of shapes and colours, keeping the pattern fairly simple. Repeat the process with the remaining three lengths of fabric.

When the painted fabric lengths are completely dry, cut them in half lengthways so you end up with eight pieces, 3 m (10 ft) long and 60 cm (2 ft) wide. At the top of each piece, fold over 5 cm (2 in) of fabric to create a loop for the tubing. Pin and sew. If you like, hem the bottom of each length (I didn't, but I'm lazy).

Cut the irrigation tubes into one 1 m (3 ft 3 in), one 2 m (6 ft 8 in) and one 3 m (9 ft 10 in) lengths. Join the ends of the 2 m (6 ft 8 in) length together with tubing joiners to form a hoop. Repeat for the 3 m (10 ft) length.

Feed the 1 m (3 ft 3 in) length of tube through the loops at the top of each fabric length, ensuring the painted side of the fabric is facing outwards. Fasten with a joiner.

163

Place the hoops in order of size, starting with the smallest in the centre (the smallest hoop will have all the fabric attached). Using a tape measure, measure and mark eight equally distanced spaces around the hoops: 1 m (3 ft 3 in) hoop = 12.5 cm (5 in); 2 m (6 ft 6 in) hoop = 25 cm (10 in); 3 m (9 ft 10 in) hoop = 37.5 cm (15 in).

Align the ends of the four lengths of rope, then fold them in half and tie in a knot at the folded end, leaving loops at the top for hanging. Tie the eight ends of rope at the marked spaces on the hoops, starting at the top hoop and moving down to the next marked line on the next hoop, so the rope stays in line. Leave 20 cm (8 in) of rope between the top knot and the smallest hoop, 25 cm (10 in) between the small and medium hoop, and 30 cm (12 in) between the medium and largest hoop. Trim any excess rope. Hang from the nearest shady spot using a lasso knot.

YOU WILL NEED:

- handsaw
- 30 cm (12 in) length of 25 mm (1 in) wide dowel (keep any spare dowel for back up)
- electric drill
- 8 mm (⅜ in) and 14 mm (½ in) drill bits
- vice (optional)
- fine-grit sandpaper
- cloth or rag
- pencil
- small paintbrush and paint
- varnish
- 2.1 m (7 ft) of cotton rope

SKIPPING ROPE

Although I sucked at elastics and was constantly 'it' in tiggy, I would list skipping rope at the top of my schoolyard prowess. I would happily skip for days, and was even pretty handy at the occasional trick – I could do 'criss-cross' and 'side swing' with my eyes closed, although I never did manage to master the 'double Dutch'.

When I had finished this project, Ari wandered into my studio, picked up the rope and, to my complete surprise, asked, 'What is this?' I pretty much fell into a pile of parenting failure there and then! But we have since changed that. His technique leaves much to be desired, but he definitely has the skipping bug. I'm now on a one-woman crusade to bring the skipping rope trend back to the schoolyard!

NOTE: The length of rope used in this project is enough to make a skipping rope for one adult. If you would like to make a bigger rope for multiple people to jump with, or a smaller rope for a smaller person, simply increase or decrease the length of the rope. For eight-year-old Ari, I decreased the length of the rope by 20 cm (8 in).

Using the handsaw, cut the dowel into two 15 cm (6 in) pieces.

Using the drill and the 8 mm (⅜ in) drill bit, drill a hole through the length of both pieces of dowel. The drill bit won't fit the whole way through the dowel, so drill one end halfway and then turn the dowel over and drill from the other end.

168

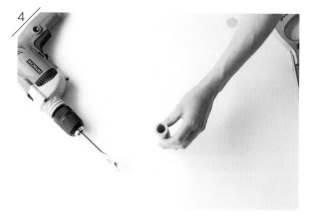

TIP: Drilling the dowel can be tricky, so if at first you don't succeed, try and try again. Securing your dowel in a vice can help to keep the hole even when drilling.

Using the 14 mm (½ in) drill bit, drill a wider hole in one end, about 5 cm (2 in) deep, which will allow enough space for the knotted rope to fit inside the dowel.

Sand the dowel and edges until smooth, then dust off with the cloth.

Using the pencil, draw your design onto the dowel pieces. Keep the design fairly simple, using patterns such as waves, stripes or dots.

Paint your design. Once dry, apply a coat of varnish.

Thread the rope into one piece of dowel, starting at the end with the smaller hole. Push the rope through to the end with the wider hole, then pull it through and knot tightly. Pull the rope down so the knot sits neatly inside the wider end of the dowel. Repeat for the other end of the rope and remaining piece of dowel.

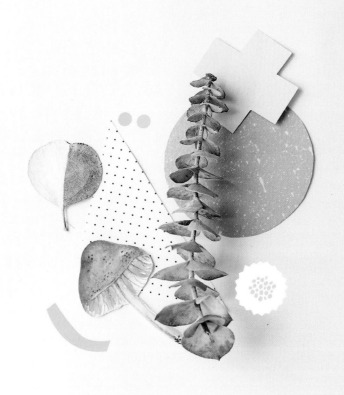

YOU WILL NEED:

- pencil and paper
- a large vessel (I used a large enamel baking dish that I bought from an op shop and drilled holes in the bottom for drainage)
- a variety of small plants with varying heights, colours and widths (work out if your garden will be inside/outside/in the shade/full sun, and buy plants accordingly – bonsai plants can work well)
- potting mix
- small trowel
- a variety of mosses (I gathered moss from the alleyways behind my house and kept it very moist and in a dark spot until I needed it)
- rocks for stepping-stone path
- pebbles (I used 2 different sizes: very small and tiny)
- 12–15 toothpicks for fence
- scraps of fabric and small twigs for teepee

MINI GARDEN

Earlier this year I was asked to decorate a doll's house for a charity auction. I loved it so much and spent way too much time re-covering tiny sofas, making tiny cushions and a tiny balsa-wood bookshelf with tiny versions of my books sitting on the shelves. Things got a tiny bit out of control! If I didn't have a deadline to get it finished, I would have spent all my time on it. I could have happily made it my new career.

Once the doll's house went off to its new home, I realised a few things: 1. The seven-year-old child inside of me is still alive and well. 2. I've never gotten over my love for all things miniature. 3. There was a giant hole left in my life where the doll's house project had been ... So, I moved on to the next miniature thing I could get my hands on – a miniature garden. I made this at home, and Ari loved it so much he made one as well. It's a really great project to do with kids.

Draw out a loose plan for your mini garden. Decide where the different plants will sit, how the path will work, where the small pebbles will go and where the teepee will sit.

Pot the larger plants in the vessel first, adding extra potting mix under and around the plants as needed.

176

If you are using moss, gently press it into the dirt around the plants, remembering to leave space for the path.

Using the rocks, make a stepping-stone path.

Add the small and tiny pebbles around the path and any areas around the plants and moss where the dirt is showing.

To make the fence, stick the toothpicks into the dirt. Trim the length of the toothpicks if required. Place the toothpicks in a line, spacing them fairly close together so they resemble a fence.

To make the teepee, break or cut three twigs so they are even in length. Wind a thin strip of fabric around the top of the twigs to hold them in place.

Cut a piece of fabric and wrap it around the twigs to create a cover. Secure the fabric in place by tying a strip of fabric around the top. Trim the fabric as required. Place the teepee in the garden by gently pressing the twigs into the moss and dirt.

TIP: Let your imagination run free. You could also add a swing, wishing well, campfire, seat and faux mushrooms.

178

179

YOU WILL NEED:

- clean, dry rocks in various shapes and sizes (find them in the street or park, or buy them from your local nursery)
- paper and pencil
- small paintbrushes
- acrylic paints
- eraser
- varnish (optional)
- assorted supplies for trims and extra details: felt, ribbon, small pompoms, wool, card
- scissors
- PVA glue

PET ROCKS

When I was young, I spent a disproportionate amount of time collecting rocks and putting faces on them. Googly eyes were one particular favourite touch. At one stage, I set up a street-side stall trying to fob them off. So when it came to making these guys, I had a lot of experience to draw from, except this time there wasn't a googly eye in sight. These guys are a 'Beci-2017' version.

The best thing about pet rocks is they are so EASY to make. You could dress them up to look like your friends, members of your family or even your pets (there's definitely a Tio in there). Spend time planning what (or who) you'll paint on your rocks, matching their shapes to different personalities. You will be rewarded with extra good-looking rocks if you do.

Spread your rocks out on a work table and look at their shapes and sizes. Sketch out some rough ideas for each rock.

Use a pencil to draw your designs on the rocks.

1 /

2 /

182

3 /

4 /

Using the small paintbrushes and paints, paint in the larger areas, such as the eyes, the hair or a hat.

Once the paint is dry, paint in the details such as the eyeballs, nose and mouth. If you can still see pencil lines, once the paint has dried use an eraser to rub them out. If you like, finish with a coat of varnish.

Work out what trims you'd like to add to give your rocks a bit of 3D fun.

You could cut small ears or tails from felt scraps, make small bows from ribbon, braids from wool or add a small pompom to the top of a hat or for a nose.

5/

6/

7/

8/

Glue the trims to the painted rocks.

If you like, create a home for your pet rocks. They are particularly fond of beds of soft, small-leaved foliage.

TEMPLATES

MACRAMÉ CHAIR

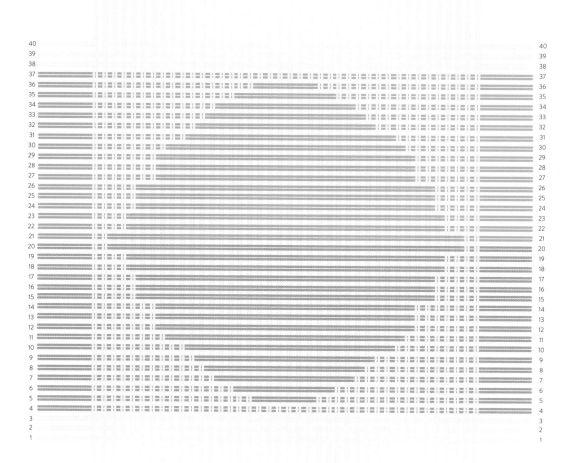

CANVAS HAMMOCK: COW HITCH KNOT

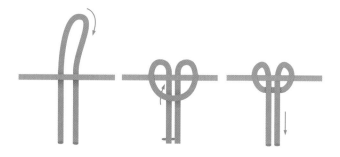

PAPER CRYSTALS: LARGE CRYSTAL

INCREASE BY 250%
WILL GO ACROSS TWO A3 PAGES

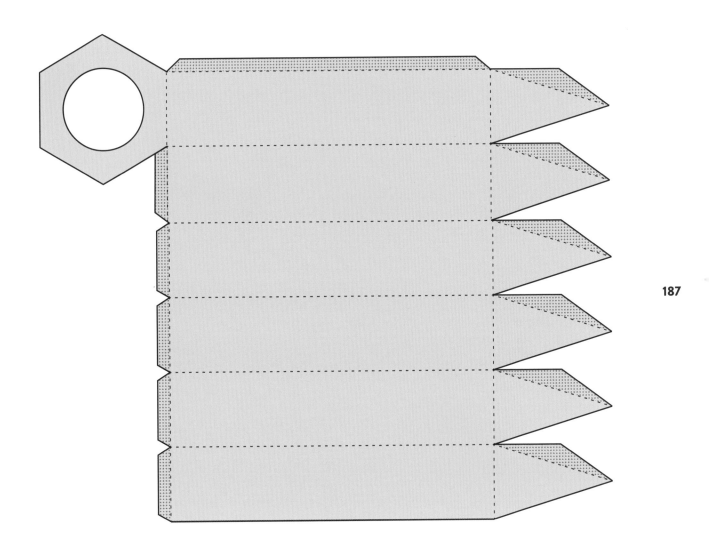

STICK

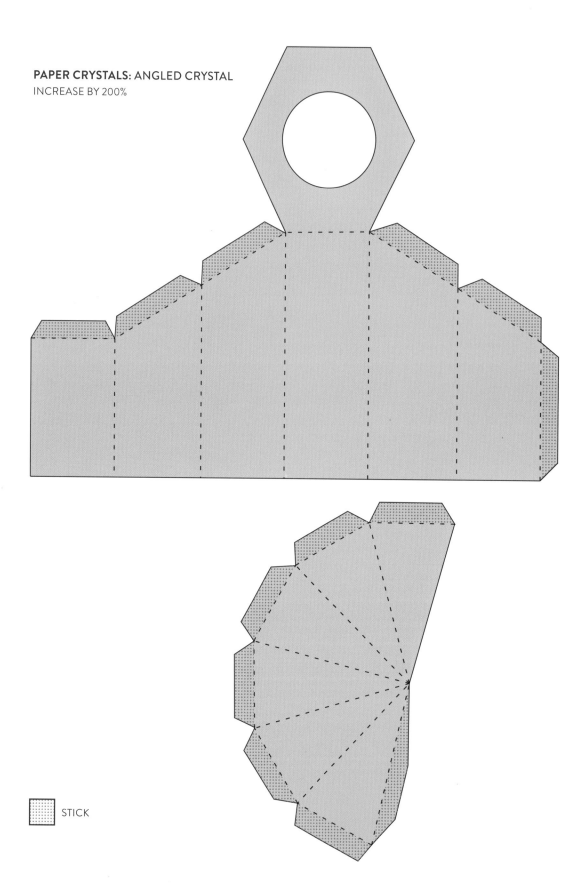

PAPER CRYSTALS: ANGLED CRYSTAL
INCREASE BY 200%

188

STICK

INCREASE BY 200%

189

STICK

Thank you

Huge thanks to Michelle Mackintosh for enduring book number four with me – I could never imagine doing this without you! You make everything so amazing, both life and books! Also thanks to Brontë and Steve.

Chris Middleton, for once again producing the best photos in the most chilled-out way there is.

Fran Berry, Loran McDougall, Vaughan Mossop and Mark Campbell at Hardie Grant – thanks for putting up with my annoying way of doing things again! Kim Rowney, for meticulous editing once again.

Taryn Rae, for being my go-to gal for all things *Sunshine Spaces*! You were a powerhouse and the best! Thanks also for your expertise and persistence with the Macramé Chair, Hiding Space and Concrete Planters projects.

My DIY interns – there was no way I could get this book done without lots of volunteers. Huge thanks to those who helped me develop and make all the projects: Nyssa Skorji (paper genius!), James Reynolds, Brianna Wall, Sophie Banh, Noni Simmons, Holly Leonardson, Cassie Byrnes, Esther Olsson and Elska Sandor.

Katie Kelso, for being such a babe and all-round lovely human being. Thanks for letting us drape all kinds of weird plant life all over you for the sake of a good photo.

Tim Orpin, for the use of his incredible gardens at Kenloch. Thanks for letting us take over and make magic.

Katie Marx and Greg Hatton, for the use of Butterland (again), and Hazel, Minnie and Rosie for being picture-perfect models.

Sarah Beaumont at Babylon Flowers, thank you for your advice and help.

Seamus Ashley at XO Studios, for turning a blind eye when we went over time – and for having the best studios!

Raph and Tyke and Ari, for living through ANOTHER book (I wasn't even that stressed this time, huh?). Also, thank you to BBK, Taco Truck, All Day Donuts and Juanita Peaches staff, particularly Van, Shane, Ed, Chris, James and Lina for putting up with the crazy mess and keeping me happy and fed.

All my great freelance clients, past and present, for being understanding while I possibly put your work on hold to work on book stuff (and for giving me jobs in the first place).

Jeremy Wortsman and the rest of the Jacky Winter crew. Risa Nakazawa and everyone at A-Gent Tokyo.

Sally Wilson, for her plant-spiration and letting me use the photos of her beautiful plant room for the Indoor Plants section (pages 42; 47; 48, bottom left).

The following shops for letting me borrow their goods: Hunting for George, Grandfather's Axe, After Store, Third Drawer Down and Gorman.

My friends who made the trek up to the Dandenongs for the day and were then willingly photographed: Meadow Picnic – Indi, Ned, Ralph (Kelly and Cam), Lulu and Ruby (Aaron and Jana); Equinox Dinner – Matt, Carly, Chrissie, French, Sam, Daisuke, Cassie, Taryn, James, Martin, Esther, Katie, Alice, Chris, Myles and Joseph.

Michael Kewish, for assisting on my second shoot and also being a step-in model. Thank you for being helpful and gorgeous.

My other brilliant friends, who keep me sane and whom I haven't yet mentioned: Ed, Liv, Milo and Fia; Shauna, Misha, Odi and Tavi; Nat and Frank; Michelle, Andrew, Bella and Guthrie; Nadia; Tory and Gabe from Splendour, Byron Bay; Dee and Harry; BNWPS mum posse; Guy; Stanislava; Christie; Max, Rosie and Fred; Lisa G; Lawrence; Leah; Daniel and Emma; Simon, Mel and Iggy; Amanda, Conor, Bonnie and Corey; Lawrence; The Mayor; and all the other people I love but don't have room to write down (you know who you are).

My family: Marg, Ross, Erwin, Emily and Sean, Leslie, Rudin, Brooke, Zed and Tahlin, Johann.

The sun for shining.

RIP Andrew Billington.

Published in 2017 by Hardie Grant Books,
an imprint of Hardie Grant Publishing

Hardie Grant Books (Melbourne)
Building 1
658 Church Street
Richmond, Victoria 3121
www.hardiegrant.com.au

Hardie Grant Books (London)
5th & 6th Floors
52–54 Southwark Street
London SE1 1UN
www.hardiegrant.co.uk

A Cataloguing-in-Publication entry is available from
the catalogue of the National Library of Australia at
www.nla.gov.au

Sunshine Spaces
ISBN 978 1 74379 213 1

Publishing Director: Fran Berry
Project Editors: Loran McDougall and Rihana Ries
Managing Editor: Marg Bowman
Editor: Kim Rowney
Design Managers: Mark Campbell and Vaughan Mossop
Designer: Michelle Mackintosh
Photographer: Chris Middleton
Production Manager: Todd Rechner
Production Coordinator: Rebecca Bryson

Colour reproduction by Splitting Image Colour Studio
Printed in China by 1010 Printing International Limited